T0171359

Other publications by Dorothea are

Book:- "Chakras" Introduction to the Seven Major Energy Centers

CD:- Guided Meditation - Sacred Activation

CD:- Guided Meditation – Deep Relaxation

ENCHANTMENT IS *Yours*

A JOURNEY OF SPIRIT

DOROTHEA ORLEEN GRANT

BALBOA.
PRESS

A DIVISION OF HAY HOUSE

Balboa Press books may be ordered through booksellers or by contacting:

Balboa Press
A Division of Hay House
1663 Liberty Drive
Bloomington, IN 47403
www.balboapress.com
1-(877) 407-4847

Because of the dynamic nature of the Internet, any web addresses or links contained in
this book may have changed since publication and may no longer be valid. The views
expressed in this work are solely those of the author and do not necessarily reflect the views
of the publisher, and the publisher hereby disclaims any responsibility for them.

The author of this book does not dispense medical advice or prescribe the use of any technique
as a form of treatment for physical, emotional, or medical problems without the advice of a
physician, either directly or indirectly. The intent of the author is only to offer information
of a general nature to help you in your quest for emotional and spiritual well-being. In the
event you use any of the information in this book for yourself, which is your constitutional
right, the author and the publisher assume no responsibility for your actions.

Any people depicted in stock imagery provided by Thinkstock are models,
and such images are being used for illustrative purposes only.
Certain stock imagery © Thinkstock.

Printed in the United States of America.

ISBN: 978-1-4525-6955-0 (sc)
ISBN: 978-1-4525-6957-4 (hc)
ISBN: 978-1-4525-6956-7 (e)

Library of Congress Control Number: 2013905722

Balboa Press rev. date: 3/27/2013

Disclaimer

The insights and illuminating thought-provoking awareness in this book is an original creation channeled through the imagination, intuition, and perception of the author, and could be seen as fictitious. Names characters, places and incidents are products of the author's imagination or are used fictitiously. Any resemblance to actual events, locales or persons living and dead, is entirely coincidental.

The information in this book **cannot** to be used as a substitute for medical, or psychological treatments. Contact your medical, and mental health professionals for medical services.

Dedication

This book "ENCHANTMENT IS YOURS" is dedicated to Dorothea's Spiritual Journey; and to my ancestors who were talented shamans, healers, herbalists, farmers. To them the non-physical realm was real rather than the regular physical world. My ancestors were my first spiritual teachers in this lifetime. They assisted me in awakening to my own authentic talents, unconditional love, and compassion.

This Book
"Enchantment Is Yours"
Belongs To

. . . .

Introduction

Sometimes in life you have to decide which bridge to cross.
If you ever cross a bridge, do not destroy it,
because you might need it again.
There are no states of perfection. There can be stages of completion.
States of perception and completion are recognized by the perceiver.
To me, the invisible realm is where everything comes from,
and where everything returns; no birth,
not death, everything continues
from the invisible to the visible, and from the visible to the invisible.
Just a continuous no proving infinite cycle of realms, and
different frequencies of energy vibrations. Each has its own purpose.
Spirit, to me, is a kaleidoscope of invisible energy and information.
Invisible energy and information: spirit's data files of all its experiences.

The true nature of the heart is a patient, and loving creature.
Loving creature the heart is without taking.
Without taking, giving, giving completely.
Completely BEING a channel for giving.
Giving life completely, the heart wants to continuously become.

Preface

I celebrate my spiritual journey with this book ENCHANTMENT IS YOURS because I am grateful for my journey, and all the people I have met so far along the way. I have had a spiritual journey that has taken me on straight, green, beautiful, narrow, crooked, wide, rocky, busy, and dark paths, growing and transforming as I journeyed.

I celebrate because also along the way I have also assisted many clients and students with their chosen growth, transformation, healing and personal development, through the very successful creation of Dogca Universal Wellness, a school of Energy Healing Arts – The Shaman's Way of Healing.

I celebrate because my journey first began when I asked myself the question, "What is it I need to be doing with my talents?" I was aware I had talents, but I was not sure what to do with them. I was awakened to the answer. I awakened to consciously begin my life's purpose in 1989. I was also awakening to my own healing, growth, and personal development, which changed my awareness and life, and the lives of so many I have assisted along the way, and still continue to do so.

Not until you have awakened and found your life's compassionate purpose and share it with others, will you ever arrive completely within yourself. So far I have experienced a multi-faceted, multi-dimensional, Spiritual journey that is infinite, and filled with unconditional love, light, and joy. Sometimes some darkness comes in along the way.

I celebrate because I am grateful for the support given to me along the way. As I choose to continue on this enlightened spiritual journey, I choose to share with you from my journal's insights and awarenesses that came to my consciousness. I always kept a journal or notebook close at hand, and when mindful awarenesses came to me, I wrote them down without judgment. And years later, here I am using these seeming notes to create this book. **You can do this too.**

I hope you enjoy reading these sacred treasured notes of mine and choose to connect to the innate, authentic artist within you. You can use the blank pages after each written page to begin creating your journal for publishing some day.

Thank you so much for purchasing my book. With gratitude I give you the gift of many blessings, light, prosperity, and love. Remember, dreams can come true, miracles can happen, and the journey of spirits is infinite.

Especially for YOU!

As you take this Spiritual journey in this book, you can see these awarenesses as stepping stones, and remember that there are blank pages for you to write your own personal insights, and awareness as you go along the way.

Acknowledgment of love and blessings

Many, many thanks to my daughter Pia for her support, computer skills, assistance in editing, and all her creative efforts in assisting me with the production and creation of this book, and everything in general. Thank you to my oldest daughter Renea for giving me the most opportunity to repetitiously practice patience, unconditional love and compassion; and to my seven-year-old granddaughter Ayanna who was born on my birthday, for her entertaining companionship and mirror of wisdom.

Thank you to:

All my human spiritual teachers especially Grace, Zen Master Thich Nhat Hanh and the Monks and Nuns of Plum Village, from The Four Winds Society Dr. Alberto, Wake, Stevi, and Pier. And to my spirit guides and helpers Gagskidms. All the clients and students who chose me to assist them on their life's path. My Inca friends Roland and Pascal for their sincere unconditional expressions and mirror of love, kindness, and sincerity, from the first moment we met to the last moment I departed from their presence. My experiences with them help to improve my personal life, and the lives of others in my professional healing arts practice. My friends in the past and present Laurna, Christine, Peter, Howard, Rene, Diane, Todd, Robert, Henry, Olga, Maryann, Debbie, Shelly, Jack, Lauren, Sharon, Alison, Barbara, Marie, David, Barack, Kathleen, and Minor, for their expressions of shared kindness. And to all the other humans I met along the way who assisted me and my life positively, and negatively.

The people, places, and things you experience in life are gifts of expressed karma. Like Footsteps, they can assist in completing different steps in the circle and paths of life.

I want to thank my editor
Renée Elizabeth-Anne Rewiski for her assistance
in bringing this book to print.
The editor is an aide who massages the author's thoughts
clarifying them
while allowing the author to remain authentic
to the brilliant, original exercise.

Table of Contents

Awareness

In order to awaken others, you must be awakened yourself.
The more restricted someone becomes, the less they can create.
If someone spends their lifetime growing spiritually, mentally,
emotionally, and physically, it could not be a wasted life.
To love and be loved is to grow.

Love is about loving yourself, and sharing your love with someone.
It is not about finding someone to love, or to be your lover.
The biggest compassion and unconditional love
someone can give is to an enemy.
When your beloved hurts you hurt.
When you let love into your life, your needs can be revealed and fulfilled.
Love is the consistent commitment to the growth
and development of yourself, and your lover, if you have one.
This love is expressed regularly, and spontaneously
through acts of giving, and receiving.
A lover is a giver, and receiver.

Sometimes you might have to knock something old
down to build something new.
To love unconditionally, sometimes you have to
let go and become the artist (Heartist) from within.
It is natural that when you accomplish a dream you feel some sense of loss.
To accomplish the dream you would have given up the old, so there comes
a sense of something lost.

Change can bring you to a place that is greater, or worse.

Me is when I wake up in the morning before I look in the mirror.

Our children are an extension of ourselves.

Children are an expression of the mirror and map that they inherit

from their parents, and other ancestors,

plus the map of their own Spiritual Being, or Soul.

As a Spiritual Being, or Soul remember that you were a child too.

Date:_____

We Are All Connected

The brain is not restricted to a right, or left brain function.
The true nature of the brain is for the five
sides to completely work together.
The five sides of the brain are a mirror of Spirit, mind,
body, and the five senses. The five elements assist in the
complete construction of life's magnificent creations.
The whole brain works together to create a function of
completeness, and union, magnificent, and powerful
beyond measure; infinitely evolving in no time.

Believing we are different is a limitation of our ego mind.
Ego mind's many disguises are of an inflated
self that is fearful of leaving its wounded restrictive space.
A mind that has experienced journeys too perilous to
trust, and too harmful to hope, creates a map of all its
perceived experiences, both positive and negative.
The mind, from its fearful awareness, creates a perceived separate
existing self that is different, maybe worse, and maybe better.
The mind's limitation restricts the creation of positive
feelings from coming in; controlling, and
suppressing negative emotional
expressions to create a safer place for the person to be.
Always know that you can move beyond the restrictions
to find a way to release the negative experiences, and

energy of the past, evolving and transforming into an
interconnected being of abundant joy, love, and light.
Finding a healing arts tool to energetically clear negative
emotions, and imprints can assist in moving beyond the restrictions.
Creating, and experiencing unconditional love,
and compassion can assist the natural
healing system of the body in repairing,
and rewiring its energy systems.
This, over time, can assist in repair and renewal
of brain, spirit, body and mind.

As the body heals itself to a place of positive
balance, the body's chemistry can also
improve. Improved bodily functions can create positive
balance for transforming negatively perceived emotions
that affected spirit, mind, body, and brain.
When the mind and body are healed and purified,
life can be experienced more harmoniously, positively, and more completely.
The body's inner divine intelligence assisted by the heart's
chakra center can assist the brain's natural ability to navigate
constructively. The brain navigating constructively, like the steering
wheel of a car, can assist in creating a more balanced state,
constructively transforming as the journey
continues to infinitely unfold.

The natural states of the spirit, mind, and body are to work from inside to
outside. The inside action it then mirrors to an
outside action, experience, and function.
When these functions completely work in balance,
together they connect us to all of life,

and all living things collectively in the
Universe. Our connectedness assists
us in an effortless journey of experiencing the power of the creator from
within us. When humans can arrive at a place
of positive harmonious love and light
they can then become the Artist they were meant to be.
The artist can create its heart's desires unbounded through joy, and chosen
arts of creative tools. Creative tools are available to all living beings.
We are all created authentically as magnificent artists.

Choosing to hide from our negative emotions
and thoughts, feeling that school
and degrees makes us who we are or what we can become, can create
a separation from our creative nature, a separation from the natural
interconnectedness of all living things, from discovering our talents,
and infinite resources within.

Teachers assist us in remembering what is already inside us.
Everyone was born with the same potential of the creator's divine
resources, and blessings from within.
So let us start to become best friends to ourselves, and love
ourselves unconditionally; then expend these gifts to others.
Remember if one person can master the journey, we all have the
potential to do the same, because we are all connected.

Believe anything with all your heart and you can dream it into being.
Use light and love as your tools of creation, and remember to
enjoy the journey. You are the instrument. The musical energy from
within you is free, and will freely play with you.

The next time you look in the mirror please know that you are
NOT limited to the reflection you perceive in the mirror.
The YOU perceived in the mirror from within is a divine projected
image of the master creator, who created you
in its own image and likeness.
You are collectively connected to a mirror and likeness of
Source that is nameless, too large, and too deep to measure.
Too divine to restrict, a knowing you should treasure.

Know that you are an artistic creator, a mirror of Universal Source. .
Enchanted you are. Enchantment you will always be.
Stop now and enjoy the divine creation that is YOU.
Feel the journey from within, and let it
collectively shine through as an
enchantment of creative Universal Life Force Energy; a gift of Source.

Welcome to your enchanted journey of your life.
Your life to experience; feel it and enjoy.
ENJOY YOU!
Enchantment Is Yours

Date:_____

_____

_____

_____

_____

_____

_____

_____

_____

_____

_____

_____

Love Shared

When you made love to me, my whole being,
especially my body, would melt like butter in hot sun.
I could feel you penetrating my whole being,
like sunbeam penetrating rose buds before they open up
into magnificent flowers.
I experienced your gentleness kindness,
sentimental touches, and peace arrived effortlessly.
I felt your kisses deep inside me, like seeds opening
up after being marinated by the dark
moist earth, taking root into every part of my body, and soul.
When I looked into your eyes, stars bloomed magnificently,
like a sky filled with stars on a full moon night.
I would melt with joy in your arms, like orange yellow
peaches succulent from ripening in the hot sun.
Your spirit and my spirit merged as one.
Your mind and my mind looked into the mirror of its essence.
Your body and my body danced to the beat of
our hearts, like drummers drumming around a bonfire.
Inside, and outside we merged like ocean and sand.
I adored you; a priceless gift of love shared.

Date:_____

_____

_____

_____

_____

_____

_____

_____

_____

_____

_____

_____

_____

Seduction

Seduction by and of spirit is the highest seduction.
Once the tango dance of one spirit and the other spirit begins,
the mind must, and will surrender willingly for each person
to connect to their hearts. This is the highest and most
divine bonding in relationship. This connection can
only be made through love's divine intervention. A match
made in heaven, and passionate bliss.
With spirits, love, light, and soul, now the tango of no mind
continues. The spirit with the most light egolessly leads the way.
The tango of healing, and purification continues, giving
each mind the opportunity to heal slowly; step by step
the tango continues. Bonding, and growing, evolving
and knowing, each spirit's heart, soul, mind, and body unite.
Evolving back to a separate union, the joyful seduction
of spirits independently experience new delightful beginnings.
New delightful beginnings for seduction of self continue.

Date:_____

_____

_____

_____

_____

_____

_____

_____

_____

_____

_____

_____

True Friendships

True friendships are like mountains and diamonds.
Together as the friendship evolves they
create harmony, love, light, and beauty
for the friendship, and others, collectively.
Unconditionally this ship journeys from
destination to destination, and through life's ups,
and downs, without any frown.
Caring without any frown, the friendship carries the
friends from shore to shore.

Date:_____

_____

_____

_____

_____

_____

_____

_____

_____

_____

_____

_____

# See You

I see you from within the depth of your eyes, your soul, and your heart.
Your eyes, your soul, see me from within the depth of your heart.
Our spirits see each other completely, through the depths
of our eyes, soul, heart, mind and body.
Within your spirit and eyes I see YOU.

Date:_____

_____

_____

_____

_____

_____

_____

_____

_____

_____

_____

_____

_____

Light

O see the light Power.

Feel it when you touch.

Feel it when you talk.

Feel it when you walk.

See the sun see the moon power.

Embrace feel it, kiss, touch feel it.

Magnificent, divine light power.

Darkness, so black so still.

Enters light, so light.

Movement, security, feel it, power.

Come in, step into the light.

Light opens your mind, body, and soul, feel it.

Soak it in, from within, sing rejoice, feel it Power.

Beauty is light mixed with fearless darkness.

One cannot exist without the other.

From Darkness came light, from night comes light.

Need each other exists as one helping the other power.

Light and darkness can create power.

Only together feel it.

Date:_____

_____

_____

_____

_____

_____

_____

_____

_____

_____

_____

_____

Cosmic Dance

Passionately, the wind dances across the
island in majestic twirling essence.
The coconut trees sway from side to side, and
bow to its caressing interlude.
The smell of the salty air, and the lapping of the ocean waves echoes.
Overhead the full moon gave off a majestic
glow of grounded illumination.
Stars lit the sky like sprinkled confetti. In
the background, the dark blue-
grey sky flowed softly with few fluffy clouds.
The night's enchanting performance continues. The tide rises. It is safe.
The ocean keeps up its vibration of ebb and flow. Rising and falling as
it keeps the planet on the right vibration, back and forth.
The humans nestle in for a night of rest. It feels safe for the sea turtles,
crabs, and other sea creatures to come on shore.

The night continues its musical, illustrious performance.
Soon it will be sunrise. Soon the light, the big fire will come.
The night will rest. From the east like a flicker of low but bright
light peeking out from the ocean floor, comes the sun,
the big light, the big fire. The sun rises slowly, as if lifting itself up, and up.
The sun lighting up the ocean into colors of rich blues, greens, and grays.
The sky is now transformed into colors of red, orange, yellow, green, pink,
light blue, deep blue, and purple. White clouds in the background complete
the scene. The sky is one picturesque rainbow. Everything smiles.

The ocean pulls back; the ocean rests. The sea turtles and other sea creatures return to the ocean. Crabs dig fresh holes in the sand to retreat in for the day. The wind rests; it subsides to a gentle fresh breeze. The moon and stars becomes invisible, disappearing into the sky. The sun has fully risen to a magnificent bright yellow, brightly beaming, nurturing energetic glow.

Human life comes slowly awake, alive.

The sun caresses all of life. The cosmic dance continues.

Date:_____

Ultimate Unconditional Love

Ultimate unconditional love has no beginning or end.
It spins like a wheel creating a backward and forward
movement of unconditional acceptance of love.
The circular part of the wheel is feminine, and the straight
lines within, are masculine. Together they create a dance
that assists the wheel in moving. Ultimate unconditional
love is pure magnificent complete union of spirit and light.

Date:_____

_____

_____

_____

_____

_____

_____

_____

_____

_____

_____

_____

_____

Love is

Love is caring. Not fearing.
Love is kind.
Not blind.
Love is wet. Not upset.

Bless Your Lover

Bless your lover as he retires to dreamland.
Wish him or her safe journey on entering dreamland.
May he or she awaken to fresh joy of another sunny day.
Another sunny day to laugh, and to play.

Date:_____

Journey of Love

The journey of love flows like water rolling,
and strolling down a stream filled with
diamond, emerald, ruby, precious things.
Flowing along like the wind, the journey
of love begins and continues.

Date:_____

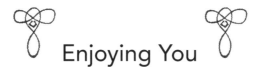

Enjoying You

I am enjoying you. I am enjoying you talking to me.
Me, I drink your words in like cool champagne.
Like cool champagne I am enjoying you.

Date:_____

_____

_____

_____

_____

_____

_____

_____

_____

_____

_____

_____

_____

Soul Mates

Like fresh rain after a hot summer day, soul mates
transcend, and connect. Bringing new
life, new smiles, sensuous breeze through
their spirit, mind, and body.
Boy, girl, baby, man, or woman, one or
the other it does not matter.
Connect, and sing to the meeting of spirit, soul and matter.

Date:_____

_____

_____

_____

_____

_____

_____

_____

_____

_____

_____

_____

_____

Sharing Love

To share love is to know love.
If the nurturing energy of love was never known and experienced
by the giver, and receiver, then the giver and receiver
of love cannot know how to give and receive authentic nurturing love.
The love given and experienced will be a mirror of fearful experiences
from within, transferring these vibrations back and forth.
Back and forth frictions within, and to the other, like thunder, clashing,
rolling, and falling forward, and backward, the love will be experienced.
To know love is to share love.
To share love is to know love.

Date:_____

_____

_____

_____

_____

_____

_____

_____

_____

_____

_____

_____

_____

I Love You Because

I have plenty of Love to give.

Spending time with you gives me the opportunity to see myself.

When I am with you I feel I receive the

opportunity to grow, and evolve more.

You are interesting.

I see and feel a magnificent beautiful spirit that wants to grow.

Our spirits have chosen each other to transform and evolve.

You have the ability to assist me, and I have the ability to do the same.

I feel safe in your company. My spirit loves your spirit.

My spirit is always on a quest for growth and transformation,

and has chosen a great teammate to do so with.

The dynamics of your spirit, mind, and body

sometimes can be challenging,

and my spirit, mind, and body like the challenge, and are enjoying

the opportunity. I experience your gentleness,

compassion and kindness,

even when you seem not to be aware of being this way.

I can connect to the love within you.

I love you unconditionally because we are interconnected,

like the light in the sun, the moon and the stars.

I love you because you are you.

Date:_____

_____

_____

_____

_____

_____

_____

_____

_____

_____

_____

_____

_____

_____

The Heart

What is more important than knowledge?
More important than knowledge are
the things that make life worth living.
Things that cannot be thought of in the mind,
but rather they must be felt in the heart.

Date:_____

_____

_____

_____

_____

_____

_____

_____

_____

_____

_____

_____

_____

Love Can Be

Love can be unselfish and unconditional.
Like planting a seed in the earth and taking care of it.
A close friendship that supports safe passage from
one destination to another.
An empty space, a void that will keep you warm
when things gets cold.
It is also physical erotic expressions telling the other
person that you are completely present.
Love is infinite, a warm empty void waiting
for you to be refilled again, and again.
Love refills you again and again.
True LOVE can never die.
Never dies, and never ends.

Date:_____

_____

_____

_____

_____

_____

_____

_____

_____

_____

_____

_____

_____

Longing

My beloved, where are you tonight?
In my dream I caress your face, and
then your whole body.
I am longing for you to return home.
Home in my arms.

Sense

When something does not make
sense, this is when it makes the most sense

Date:_____

_____

_____

_____

_____

_____

_____

_____

_____

_____

_____

_____

_____

Hot Wet Wild

I feel your presence.
Your presence penetrates my soul.
My heart opens spontaneously, like ocean breeze
caressing palm trees on a romantic moon-lit night.
On a romantic moon-lit night, inside and outside
my body trembles with excitement.
So warm, so hot, so wet the feeling of your presence
swirls all around me. I smell the sweet fragrance
of your manhood; all my senses, come alive, awake.
I shiver with wild excitement, like wet grass bathed by the
rain and sunlight.
As I dream awake about you. Hello; are you here?
Or are you there?

Date:_____

His Eyes

In his eyes I see the stars.
In his eyes I see his heart. In his eyes I see his soul.
In his eyes I see the galaxy.
In his eyes I see the temple of the cosmos.
In his eyes I see my eyes.
In his eyes a mirror of everything.
In his eyes I see everything.

Date:_____

I Recognize You

I recognize you through your eyes.
Your eyes recognize me through your soul.
Your soul knows that I have a piece of the
puzzle that it needs to fulfill its destiny.
To fulfill my destiny, my soul recognizes
that you have a piece of the puzzle that I need to
fulfill my destiny. Our destinies recognize each other.
We recognize each other

Date:_____

_____

_____

_____

_____

_____

_____

_____

_____

_____

_____

_____

_____

Love Is Stardust

Love is universal, and an expression of warm
caring, limitless joy, and creative feeling.
Love can be sprinkled into expressions of stillness, or
experiences of movement and looking, like a glance, a touch, listening,
and hearing, an intension of passionate erotic adventure,
starburst of deep ecstasy and passion, and deep watery oceanic vibrations.
Vibrations arriving at a magical destination of being deeply connecting
to yourself, and everything else.
Like rainbow and stardust, sprinkle love around like confetti,
and smile as you shine. Smile as you shine; love is stardust.

Date:_____

_____

_____

_____

_____

_____

_____

_____

_____

_____

_____

_____

_____

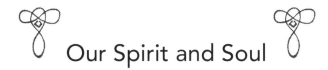

Our Spirit and Soul

My spirit and soul are touched by the call of your spirit and soul.
We are kindred spirits and souls. Our spirits and souls know each
other, and came together to grow, and to play.
My mind is touched by your mind. Your mind
is touched by my mind. Our minds together
are similar, different, compatible, and complementary.
Our spirits and souls are unique in combination, too rare to measure.

When our minds experience each other, our
Being expands, but some parts of your mind resists.
Your mind is fearful, it wants to be careful.
Please mind, Oh PLEASE LISTEN!, he yearns to be free,
let him be, to open from within, so he can sing.
His soul knows that I have what it needs
to grow and expand. So give him space to
find his grace, so he can fulfill his desired destiny with taste.

When our spirits connect, everything is amplified.
His Being expands, my Being expands.
Our destiny is somehow entangled.
Together seeing, and feeling the exchange, and expansion of spirits
your mind quivers, but your heart, and soul
get a chance to peek through,
to be lit by the light of our spiritual embrace of each other.

Oh mind, please do not fear or shed a tear, I will take care.

I feel, I see, I smell, I taste, and I touch an invisible

mirror, so, so much an exchange, too rare to touch,

to grasp, too precious, too wholesome to miss.

I long to kiss your eyes, I long to kiss your soul, and your heart.

One day your mind will become secure, I am sure.

Until then, my spirit, my mind, and my body will wait

patiently for your mind to become confident and content.

Maybe then your mind will let go, and be able to trust.

Trust so much that you can completely experience

the union of your spirit, soul and heart, for yourself, then us.

A journey of the Beloved returning once more, again, and again

to renew, to grow, to play, to experience a complete destiny too

large to measure, and pleasures to treasure.

If your mind still resists I will not persist. I will remain your bosom
friend to the end, as I continue to attend to my divinity, and my destiny
of sharing my love, light, and peace of spirit, and soul.

Date:_____

_____

_____

_____

_____

_____

_____

_____

_____

_____

_____

_____

_____

Spiritually Loving

One does not give their heart away when they are spiritually loving.
In spiritual love you share your heart, like an energy exchange.
It is like the sun sharing its heart of love, and light to all living things.
In doing so, it does not loose itself; it becomes lighter, and brighter.
Shining happily, giving unconditionally to everything.
In spiritual loving, the love and light of the union is joined in bonding
together, reflecting back to each other, assisting
in the evolution, growing more
beautiful, and stronger. Nothing is ever lost
in the exchange on the journey
of unconditional love and authentic friendship.
The two become a mirror.
Inside to outside, outside to inside, like a mirror reflecting
back unto itself is spiritual loving

Date:_____

_____

_____

_____

_____

_____

_____

_____

_____

_____

_____

_____

_____

Sweet Rose

I long for your presence so
much my body aches.
The yearning, longing,
and throbbing sensation
blossomed into the fragrance
of sweet rose dew drops.

Date:_____

_____

_____

_____

_____

_____

_____

_____

_____

_____

_____

_____

To Love Is To Evolve

Love spelled backwards is evol (ve)
to make the love evolution even more extended,
boundless, and limitless, add friendship, respect, honor,
loyalty, trust, light, and expansion.
When you say "I love you" to someone, it
means I will grow with you, and I value
you as much as I love, and value myself.
Be my mirror, I am committed to being your mirror.
Love is the mirror of evolving, growing, and awakening.
Awakening to love to evolve.

Date:_____

_____

_____

_____

_____

_____

_____

_____

_____

_____

_____

_____

_____

Where Are You Tonight

My sleepless nights I lay awake.
I lay awake dreaming of our first embrace,
and our first kiss, which I miss.
I remember kissing you and licking your neck,
sucking on your ears, and kissing your eyes.
I miss you my beloved.
I miss you like the sun misses its light.
Like the rainbow misses its colors.
It is now night and the moon beams light up my heart.
Beloved, I wonder, where, where are you tonight.

Date:_____

# Love

Love is when one steps outside of himself or herself to unite
with someone or something that mirrors itself.
Some of the main ingredients are
love, trust, faith, light, forgiveness,
patience, compassion, and being available for the
energy to enjoy passionately flowing through the selves.

Date:_____

_____

_____

_____

_____

_____

_____

_____

_____

_____

_____

_____

_____

Being In Love

To Love is to surrender.

Surrender to being open.

Being open for the energy of love.

The energy of love to flow freely.

Flow freely through you and in you.

You being in love is aligning with source.

Aligning with source creates a mirror of stupendous
creativity and joy.

Creativity and joy to share.

Date:_____

_____

_____

_____

_____

_____

_____

_____

_____

_____

_____

_____

_____

Loving Endlessly

Loving endlessly like — farming:
cultivating the earth, planting seeds, allowing seeds to grow
into food for nourishment and sustenance.
Love is endless fuel, smiling, warmth, two eyes, two hands,
two feet, nose smelling, two ears listening,
taste buds tasting, two hearts touching, two
breasts filled with milk waiting for the baby to be fed.
Loving endlessly is the pulsating vibration of wisdom
and intelligence creating everything endlessly and infinitely loving endlessly.

Date:_____

Falling In and Out of Love

Falling in love can evolve into unconditional
love but most of the time you
can fall and hurt yourself, and the other person too.
Falling in and out of love can
be experienced as warm, hot, cold and frozen.
Falling in love is falling.

Date:_____

_____

_____

_____

_____

_____

_____

_____

_____

_____

_____

_____

Love and Erotic

Love does not need erotic.
Erotic does not need love.
Love can be one of the expressions of erotic.
Erotic can be one of the expressions of love.
If someone enjoys love with someone
else it does not mean erotic.
If someone enjoys erotic with someone
it does not mean love.
Love and erotic can tango together,
like sun and cloud, moon and stars, waves and sand.
Love and erotic are endless companions.
Companions to share is love and erotic.

Date:_____

_____

_____

_____

_____

_____

_____

_____

_____

_____

_____

_____

_____

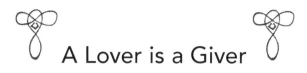

A Lover is a Giver

Love is the consistent commitment
to the growth of yourself
and the other, expressed regularly
and spontaneously through acts of giving.
A lover is a giver.

Date:_____

_____

_____

_____

_____

_____

_____

_____

_____

_____

_____

_____

_____

_____

Creative Love

To Love is to surrender. Surrender to being open.
Being open for the energy of love,
the energy of love to flow freely.
Flow freely through you and in you. You being in
love is aligning with Source.
Aligning with Source creates a mirror of stupendous
creativity and joy. Creativity and joy to share.

Date:_____

Fasting of Friendship

Some suggestions of mindfulness tips for the
fasting of friendship journey are:
Give time sometimes instead of taking time away.
If you get cold, drink some warm water.
If that does not work, put on a sweater or sweatshirt.
If you get hot, open your windows. If that
does not work, take a cold shower.
Each morning you wake up before you open your eyes and
get out of bed, close one of your hands and tap three times
on your heart, to let your heart know you are there.
When you take a shower look up at the ceiling
for eleven seconds before you start.
Wiggle your toes every now and again. Sometimes
turn on some music and dance.
Sing every now and again, even if it is "twinkle twinkle little star."
Wiggle your fingers use your left hand to shake your right hand.
Look in the mirror when you brush your teeth
and the toothpaste is dripping, then smile to the
person in the mirror and say "HI Buddy!"
Eat with your fingers when you can.
Buy a ball or if you already have one, play with it.
Appreciate the other person even when they seem
unbearable. If you can't at the moment, maybe when you
get older, or when you fast him or her out of existence.

There is not time in time. Just perception of time creates time.
Fasting is healthy, and productive; it can assist in restarting the
digestive system, and awaken to higher states of consciousness.
Now here are some secrets I would like to share with you.
Bring your ears over and I will whisper it in your ear.
Remember it is very wonderful and beautiful to have a
loving, caring and kind person as a friend. To support and
carry a nourishing friendship can be a rare gem.

Things disappear when you least expect.
Remember nothing physical lasts forever.
Energy lasts forever. Once energy is created, it cannot be destroyed.
It takes more effort to transform energy from negative to positive.
Live and enjoy life in the now.
Life is a joyride with no destination.
There is another person that really cares about you.
Guess who! your best friend.
Fasting of friendship can be useful, and may be not.

Date:_____

_____

_____

_____

_____

_____

_____

_____

_____

_____

_____

_____

_____

Authentic Friend***Ship

A friend is

Someone who assists in transporting you
from one destination or situation to
another; being your company as you sail along the ocean of life.
Someone who shares your ups, and downs, your joys and sorrows.
Someone who laughs and cries with you.
One of the true virtues of a friend is someone who
respects you, and never takes advantage of you, especially
when you are vulnerable or in a weak zone.
Sees the beauty in your Being even when you
are being your worst expression of Self.
Is always there for you even when you think you cannot go on, when things
get rough. They become the motivating force behind the change you seek.
Will always choose to stay in your life even when you
seem to not want them around; waiting and checking to
see if you are ok, even when you scream "go away,
do not talk to me," they seem to sense that you do not mean it;
even when you are also creating a fasting of their friendship.
Will never take advantage of your vulnerability or use you as a game
to their selfish advantage.
Will respect your choices and space of expression even when
you are making a fool of yourself. They will try to give you
the space to learn the lessons from the seemingly foolish
experiences, or your mistakes, and help you up if you fall.

Will understand when you are not in a good mood.
Is someone when you ask them to stay away, they try,
but sometimes might not be successful at staying away,
checking in sometimes to see if you are ok,
and getting yelled at for checking.
Is someone who, if you do not speak to them
for years, when you both reconnect,
it seems like yesterday.
Does not take you for granted.
Does not hesitate to assist you when you ask for help.
A friend will do the same for themselves as they would do for you.
They will love you as much as they love themselves.
A friend is a Rare Gem, a great gift of self to another.
**A friend is an expressions of LOVE and
LIGHT on your life's journey**.
Thank you for giving me the opportunity to be your friend.

Date:_____

_____

_____

_____

_____

_____

_____

_____

_____

_____

_____

_____

Rare Moments

Rare moments are the ones that you treasure
Treasured moments are: loving yourself, loving others,
forgiveness, appreciation, opportunities to grow,
births, deaths, commitment, kindness, friendship,
assisting others, assisting all living things,
and all your artistic creations.
The rarest of moments are the enjoyment
within each moment.

Date:_____

_____

_____

_____

_____

_____

_____

_____

_____

_____

_____

_____

_____

Loving You

Loving you is like giving birth to
myself in every moment. Every moment
giving birth to myself over and over again.

Date:_____

_____

_____

_____

_____

_____

_____

_____

_____

_____

_____

_____

Appreciation

Do not wait until unforeseen circumstances occur that
take a beloved one out of your life to show appreciation.
Show love, appreciation, and gratitude for them as often as possible.
Appreciation and gratitude are priceless gifts of unimaginable wealth.
Learn to appreciate.

Date:_____

My Divinity

I completely give my divine spirit, mind, heart, soul,
and body the freedom, and flexibility, to love and to sing.
To love, and to sing from within my mind, heart,
soul and body enjoys my spirit's magnificent effortless
journey of spirit and friendship.
Spirit's divine journey is unbounded, a kaleidoscope
of creator, artist, colorful vibrations, and adventures that
evolve and begins, again and again.
Again and again I refresh my divinity.

Date:_____

_____

_____

_____

_____

_____

_____

_____

_____

_____

_____

_____

Welcome Ayanna

Thank you for coming to light your parents' way.
You are on your way like a star in the sky
Like a full moon on a pleasant night.
May your journey in your mother's womb be filled with
pleasant experiences, yummy food, restful days, heartfelt pleasantries.
May your journey as you enter this planet be effortless and interesting.
Please take time on the path of your birth to stop and smell the roses.
May Your Journey onwards after you enter the planet
be one of love, health, wisdom, creativity and prosperity.
May light and love surround you always.
My blessings be with you now and always.
May three swans be your foundation
as you journey through your life and beyond.

Date:_____

_____

_____

_____

_____

_____

_____

_____

_____

_____

_____

_____

_____

I Love Grandma

Grandma is the best, best, best girl.
She is the best girl in the whole world.
She is so cute, she is so fine.
I love my grandma all the time
She sings me songs, she buys me shoes,
she buys me trains, and she buys me books,
she tells me stories and she eases my worries.
Grandma is so warm, and she is a charm.
Nana, Nana, Nana she is so fine, she is divine.
I love my grandma all the time.
Grandma she is love, and she is a dove.
I love my grandma all the time.

Date:_____

Ego

Ego is an emotional state expressed by the person's
mind: projection and perception. The mind's many fearful
disguises protect the perceiver from perceived harm.
Ego is incuriosity and fear based, but has good intentions.
Good intentions lie within the ego to protect the person.
The ego explores fear as a navigational tool
on a divine transformational quest for love and light,

Date:_____

_____

_____

_____

_____

_____

_____

_____

_____

_____

_____

_____

Confident Perception

Perceiving things as they are comes from the perception of an
energetically purified mind and body connected to spirit.
Insecure, incomplete, in darkness, and in fear, the mind can remain
until through some intervention, it chooses to release the
perceived trauma of not feeling safe, and being in danger.
The intelligent divine wisdom of spirit, mind, and body can be
reconnected after purification to the source of confident
perception of trust, safety, love and light.
Living conscious in confident perception is unbounded
freedom of transformation, and continuous emptiness can be possible.
Yes confident perception can be possible.
Possible confident perception can be.

Date:_____

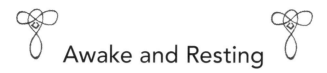 Awake and Resting

Fearless darkness in pure form can be source resting, by closing its eyes.
Light or daylight can be source being awake by opening its eyes.
Source closing its eyes resting.
Source opening its eyes awakening.
Awakening and resting continuously is source
evolving in no time, and no space.

Date:_____

_____

_____

_____

_____

_____

_____

_____

_____

_____

_____

_____

New Eyes

Dripping away the past, the windows of my eyes sadly cry.
My eyes sadly cry fresh tears like morning dewdrops awakened.
Awakened by the sun's magnificent rays of fire.
The sun's magnificent rays of fire keep changing the views of the past.
The views of the past, old adventures, creating and weaving new
dreams into creation like a magical carpet of many
eyes, like a magical carpet of peacock's feather.
Many eyes of green, blue, and black, like peacock's feather
dreaming into creation fresh mirrors of seeing new things,
and old adventures with new eyes. Smelling changes with
my new eyes I can see, and feel adventures
of my soul's and heart's desire.
Evolving, and awakening, again and again
to see and to feel with new eyes.

Date:_____

Stepping Outside Yourself

Love is stepping outside of yourself to unite with
something that mirrors oneself.
Some of the main ingredients are trust, faith, patience,
and lots of time.
You connect to the other; the other connects to you.
Love is the quest of all ages.
Love can be stepping outside of yourself.
Stepping outside of yourself to become love.

Date:_____

_____

_____

_____

_____

_____

_____

_____

_____

_____

_____

_____

_____

Inner Strength

Crabs are fragile creatures, but they can endure
and ride the mighty forces of stormy ocean waves.
Crabs are fragile creatures, but without hesitation
they scamper quickly into their holes to prevent
being swept away by the ocean's mighty waves.
They have an inner strength and guidance
of cosmic divine will, and perceptive wisdom.
Crabs are fragile creatures but their inner strength
keeps them alive, and flexible.
Alive and flexible with inner strength crabs can be.

Date:_____

_____

_____

_____

_____

_____

_____

_____

_____

_____

_____

_____

_____

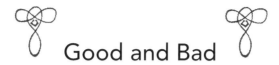

Good and Bad

People and things are not created to be good or bad.
Good or bad is a perception projected
by the experience of the individual through ego's
judgments, choices, and past experiences.
Everything has optimum potential to be empty, good, or bad.

Date:_____

_____

_____

_____

_____

_____

_____

_____

_____

_____

_____

_____

_____

Fear

Neutral, natural fear is fearless and emptiness
that can be used as a protective devise.
Fear's protective devise, void like a child in the womb,
reacts instinctively to protect itself from harm.
This kind of fear, from the cosmos' divinity, gives
protective intelligence that is necessary for survival.
Fear fearless can be absence of love.
Love is fearless of fear.
Neutral, natural fear is fearless and empty.

Date:_____

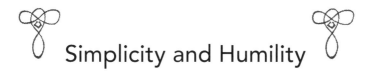

Simplicity and Humility

Everything lies within simplicity and humility.
Simplicity and humility create equanimity and peace.
Equanimity and peace create divine stillness and focus.
Divine stillness and focus create unbounded universal creativity.
Unbounded universal creativity creates divine
power for creative manifestations.
Divine manifestations can create everything.
Everything lies within simplicity and humility.

Date:_____

Turtle and Change

A turtle will be a turtle, and it loves to go within its shell.
Turtles and change do not work very well.
So do not invite a turtle to a race until it decides
through divine intervention that it
does not want to be a turtle anymore.
Remember turtles do not go fast naturally,
and they are sincere creatures of habit.
In the same way, do not try to change anyone; they
have to choose to change themselves from within.
You cannot get more out of anyone than they are willing to give.
Opportunity for change and comfort lies within humans and turtles.
Within humans and turtles lies transformation of being inside or outside.

Date:_____

To Understand

To understand yourself deeply is to understand yourself completely.

Blind

The blind man or woman sees everything. Everything sees everything blindly.

Date:_____

 Death and Rebirth

The meaning of relationship is an interaction
between something, or someone.
In a relationship, getting to a place where there is nothing left to lose but
to end the relationship is a place of pure potential, a place of death.
Death would have hit rock bottom and the only way left is up, rebirth.
If you get to this point of rebirth, know that you are in a
relationship with a lot of potential.
Know that you would have created a wheel of great
transformation, and re-awakened to love. This can be the highest
level of reconnection. Use this reconnection opportunity
to transform yourself, and the relationship. If you can
transform yourself and the relationship, do so instead of beginning
a new relationship wheel with someone else.
In a new relationship with someone else, you might end
up in the same place again.
If you are confused from reading this information,
Your relationship might be at a place of death, and rebirth.

Date:_____

Life

Life is a sport.
It is not about who wins.
It is about how you play the game
of growth, transformation, and having fun.
Life is composing creatively the
best musical composition you can experience.
Experience and explore your own creative musical notes
as you journey through life with joy.
Make joy with life.

Date:_____

_____

_____

_____

_____

_____

_____

_____

_____

_____

_____

_____

The Mind

The more empty, focused, trusting, patient,
faithful, giving, receiving, accepting, and
passionate the mind and body become,
the more fruitful abundant joy can be created
spontaneously, and synchronistically.
Like a vineyard of succulent grapes can be the mind.

Date:_____

My Blessing

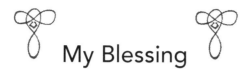

You were sent to me.
You are my angel.
You are my miracle.
It is a blessed thing to have
entered each other's life.
Thank you. I will be eternally
grateful for your presence.
One day we will wake up.
Wake up and find the real meaning
for our blessed divine union.
My blessing is your blessing.
Your blessing is my blessing.

Date:_____

_____

_____

_____

_____

_____

_____

_____

_____

_____

_____

_____

_____

Something to Nothing

Someone has everything to gain, and nothing
to lose by being in a relationship with someone.
Someone who can, or will assist in his
transformation and evolution, acts as the
mirror of the other, acting out the "why."
The person is not yours to begin with, and you are not his
to begin with; both of you at a high divine level have consciously
decided to be in each other's life unconditionally.
This is why the mirror was created in the first place.
Be grateful for the connection, and use it wisely.
Something gives rise to nothing. Nothing gives rise to something.

When there is a real need, and
there is an empty space to be filled, someone
or something rises up to fill or supply what is needed for the
empty space to be filled. Something to nothing,
and nothing to something is the authentic flow of relationship, and life.
Authentic flow of relationships and life is a mirror of nothing to something.
And also can be a mirror of something to nothing.

Date:_____

_____

_____

_____

_____

_____

_____

_____

_____

_____

_____

_____

I Look

I look and I see nothing.
I see the nothingness of the nothingness.
I see the nothingness moments of the perfection of nothing.
I see the perfection of the nothingness as a void standing still.
Standing still from within I look.
I look, and I can see moving past the silence,
voided space passing the silence from within.
Within, merging within the void, is the nothingness.
I then look again and I see an empty space.
Inside empty space, void, and nothing, I feel peace.
I look and I see nothing but peace.
I feel peace. Peace contains everything.
I look. I look. I look, and I see the nothing of peace.
The nothingness of peace standing empty, voided, and silent.

Date:_____

The Artist

Spirit is the creator's creative artist,
Artist of everything; everything is
spirit's creation, creation of everything.

Nothing

Sometimes doing nothing
is the most powerful thing to do.
To do nothing sometimes is a progressive
stillness of emptiness, peace, and nothing.

Date:_____

_____

_____

_____

_____

_____

_____

_____

_____

_____

_____

_____

To Be

To love unconditionally sometimes you have to
let go and become the artist (Heartist) from within.
It is natural that when you accomplish a dream,
you would have given up the old, so there becomes
a sense of something lost. Transformation can bring you to a
place that is greater, or worse.

Me is when I wake up in the morning before I look in the mirror.
Our children are an extension of ourselves.
Children mirror the map that they inherit from their
parents, and other ancestors, plus the map of their own spiritual being.
To be a transformed spiritual being, remember that you were a child too.
The child in you as an adult should be taken care of as well as to be.
To be the artist of unconditional love.

Date:_____

_____

_____

_____

_____

_____

_____

_____

_____

_____

_____

_____

 Birds Fly

Birds fly without fear. Without fear birds fly.
Flying without hesitation. Without hesitation birds fly.
Without hesitation you can fly.
Fly and spread your wings.
Spread your wings and fly.
Fly with wings of transformation like birds fly.

Date:_____

Your Message

I received your message.
When I received your message the night
was dark; it was after midnight.
After midnight in the darkness of the night
I could see the sun rising.
The sunrise was golden so bright
In the darkness of the night.
I was comforted by the golden sunlight in
the darkness of your message, and the night.
Is your message a dream?
In a dream I received your message.

Date:_____

Boundary

I would like to honor your request of not giving you anymore gifts.
But honoring your boundaries changes the natural
dynamics of my open heartedness, compassion, and
giving of gratitude.
So if you do not mind, I would like to be kind and honor
both our boundaries. Honor both our boundaries
by giving you an invisible gift.
A gift that you can turn into whatever you wish.
So open your hands and take my invisible gift.
Invisible gift to do whatever you wish.

Date:_____

 Illumination

Illumination is to purify the energy of trauma, clearing
the energy of fear, and finding the lost self beneath the fear.
Illuminating to become awakened to love and light,
the fountain of youth. Love and light builds up.
Darkness and fear breaks down. Illumination can be yours if you wish.

Date:_____

Leap of Faith

A leap of faith is to believe something with all your heart.
When you believe with all your heart, whatever you need can appear.
Faith opens up a window for your dreams and needs to be fulfilled.
Dreams and needs to be fulfilled by a leap of faith.
Leap of faith takes trust, and faith.
With trust and faith, you can leap.
Or you can take more time to consider the
situation of your leap of faith.

Date:_____

_____

_____

_____

_____

_____

_____

_____

_____

_____

_____

_____

_____

Responsibility

A person without responsibility sees life blindly.
When someone lays a foundation for something,
he must take the responsibility to step in,
step forward, step back, step to both sides, and
also let go. Connect to the flow of life, and on
its own, with choices unbounded, expansion can evolve.
Evolve with responsibility.

Date:_____

Sages

Great sages were not famous. In solitude they reflect.
Reflect on the lightness of emptiness and consciousness in the present.
In the present moment great sages strive to be
humble and reflect on inner wisdom.
Humility and ancient wisdom are not rationally learned.
Authentic humility and wisdom are awakened from within.
Humility is the mirror of grace and great universal power.
Great universal power gives humility and wisdom the simplicity to shine.
Shining with the power of love, and light, balanced with humility,
grace, and wisdom, you can visualize in you sages.

Date:_____

Looking

Whatever you are looking for you already have.
If you did not already have what you are
looking for, you could not perceive looking for IT.
So now my dear friends, do whatever it takes to bring what you
are looking for within and into your physical consciousness.
Your physical consciousness is visible.
Visible, to really see what you desire, by consciously looking

Date:_____

 Can You Really See

The more light you have on the path of enlightenment
the more you can see where you are, and where you are going.
The more enlightened you are when it is time to sleep, you can
close your eyes and sleep to sleep. The more
enlightened you are when you
are awake, the more awake you are to be awakened.
You will have a very restful sleep with your eyes closed, and open.
Opening to dreams will be a real awakened and enlightening
adventure to accomplish your dreams, and heart's desires.
Desires you can really see.

Date:_____

_____

_____

_____

_____

_____

_____

_____

_____

_____

_____

_____

Dead Duck Live Duck

If you were going down a path on your way home,
and there was a live duck, and a dead duck.
Which one would you take home with you?
The answer is — it depends.
Each duck can serve a different purpose.
Or maybe no duck; this has its uses too.

Date:_____

_____

_____

_____

_____

_____

_____

_____

_____

_____

_____

_____

_____

The Chicken or the Egg

Sometimes people ask: "Which comes first
the chicken or the egg?"
The answer for me is neither. The chicken and the
egg were in the same place. It just depends
on which one the person sees first,
the chicken or the egg.

Date:_____

_____

_____

_____

_____

_____

_____

_____

_____

_____

_____

_____

_____

The Way Up

The seventh realm glows with many magnificent lessons.
Lessons of countless wisdom.
Wisdom that cannot be taught.
Taught by no single way.
The Way of the path within, only the way knows
the way to teach the way.
Learning the Way is your choice.
Your choice to learn the wisdom of "The Way Up" there.

Date:_____

Change

In changing any situation you must first change yourself.
Being mindful of the change is a priceless treasure.
Change is always a refreshing treasure.
A refreshing treasure is change; change to begin anew.
To begin anew, decide consciously what to transform and change.

Date:_____

Grounding

Ground yourself into the heavens like the sky,
sun, moon, stars, other planets, clouds and lightening.
Ground yourself into the earth like the grass,
plants, trees, mountain, and the ocean kissing the earth.

Date:_____

_____

_____

_____

_____

_____

_____

_____

_____

_____

_____

_____

The Pilot

The pilot speaks freely with no hesitation,
no thinking, not inhibited by anything, the pilot speaks freely.
Like an eagle flying freely high up in the sky, the pilot
speaks and acts unbounded. Unbounded is the pilot.

Date:_____

_____

_____

_____

_____

_____

_____

_____

_____

_____

_____

_____

_____

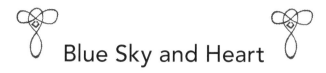

Blue Sky and Heart

An open and still mind is like a clear blue sky.
A clear and still blue sky is like the
heart and mind, clean, and conscious.
Conscious mind with rainbows can be blue sky and heart.

Dream

The mind can create from spirit
whatever you dream. Dream and create,
create and dream, this is a divine gift.
Create your dreams

Date:_____

Heart Eggs and Music

Using your heart positively teaches love.
Love is feelings of care expressed, and comes from within.
Collecting eggs teaches gentleness.
Gentleness comes from within.
Going to music school or being able to play a
musical instrument does not make one a musician.
A musician's talents come from within.
Heart, eggs, music, patience, gentleness,
and love come from within.
From within come love, gentleness, patience,
heart, eggs, and music.

Date:_____

Dreamland

Bless your lover as she retires to dreamland.
Wish your lover a safe journey in dreamland.
May your lover awaken next morning to the
fresh joy of another sunlit, refreshing day.
A refreshing day filled with memories from time in dreamland.

Date:_____

Twist & Turn

Trust the energy of the talent that speaks through
the spirit, mind, emotion, and body.
Following the energy, there are no mistakes.
Every twist, and turn, create an invisible divine formation.
An invisible divine formation surfing through the creation
like a crazy wind on a sunny raining day.
On a sunny rainy day exploring itself and caressing.
Caressing and being twisted and turned.

Date:_____

_____

_____

_____

_____

_____

_____

_____

_____

_____

_____

_____

_____

The Force of Oneness

I believe that there is a force in this Universe that lives
beneath the surface of all things. Beneath the surface of
all things is something primitive, wild, and free.
It awakens just when you need a little push, like a flower that blooms
after the wildfire turns the forest black, or like stars that smile
through a clear dark night sky.
A force that finds a way to make everything more wholesome,
bright, hot, alive and, renewed.

Some people are afraid of this force, and keep
it buried deep within their hearts,
and inside themselves. Sometimes awakening it indirectly with different
media and mirrors; afraid of direct communication, and expression
with this force. But there will always be a few people who have the
courage to love and make direct connection with this force within
themselves, and outside themselves; and to
share this connection with others.

I am one of these free-spirited people, connecting
with this force with oneness,
love, joy, passion, compassion, contentment, adventure,
peace, harmony, empowerment, balance, and freedom.
The force, set free with sacredness to roam
and explore the mountainside, and the magical
Universe like a wild mustang.

Date:_____

_____

_____

_____

_____

_____

_____

_____

_____

_____

_____

_____

The Artist

The artist is like a lover filled with light,
The creative energy of the Divine flowing through the heart;
connecting, totally trusting, stepping into the void, the
artist expresses the self that senses the expression of passion.
Merging with this flow, the artist and flow become one.
Merging with the flow and expression, both
become like a crazy wind on a sunny day.
Like a crazy wind on a sunny day exploring each other, uniting as one.
Uniting as one the artist, uniting as a nothingness void
flowing infinitely through the heart.
Merging as one are the heart and the artist.

Date:_____

_____

_____

_____

_____

_____

_____

_____

_____

_____

_____

_____

Spirit To Spirit Soul To Soul

Gently kissing my eyes, my nose, and kiss my lips.
Kiss my breast, my navel, and my hot nest of fragrant flowers.
Lips of sweet nectar juicy like peaches ripened by the hot sun.
Kiss my fingers, knees, ankles and feet.
Turn me over and kiss the bottom of my feet, behind my knees,
and all my energy centers along my spine to the top of my head.
Then turn me over again and kiss me still gently from my forehead,
my throat, heart, stomach, below my belly button to my
hot nest of fragrant flowers now flowing with the eternal lava of desire.
Then go deeper within your soul, sinking in
like water penetrating the earth
create your own burning inner desires of outward expression.
We are passionately connecting and mirroring
the sun is hot, the moon is cool,
a merging rainbow, the stars are smiling and shining brightly.
We complete the dance, a tango of a circular lock and key,
opening the door to a whole union and complete connection of, JOY!
This connection of joy is a sacred union of spirit to spirit, and soul to soul.

Date:_____

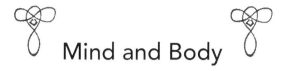

Mind and Body

When your mind and heart are connected,
when bonded in communication with me,
in your eyes I see myself.
When I see myself in your eyes,
your eyes becomes a timeless infinite mirror.
Your eyes a timeless infinite mirror of my eternal soul.
Souls connected in time. In time, lost in time, and
in no time, our mind and body unite as one.

Date:_____

_____

_____

_____

_____

_____

_____

_____

_____

_____

_____

_____

_____

Stop Now

Stop! Stop Now!
Stop and listen to nature's sounds around you.
Listen, hear the magical musical creative expressions.
Put all the sounds together. The passionate,
musical vibration of creation is calling you.
Open your heart, connect your senses,
sing and dance with great joy.
With great joy, the universe creates its manifestations.
Stop now, and listen.
Stop now.

Date:_____

_____

_____

_____

_____

_____

_____

_____

_____

_____

_____

_____

_____

Everything Shines

The sun shines, the moon shines,
the stars shine; therefore,
everything has the potential to shine.
Know that everything has the same
potential to shine. So you can SHINE!

Date:_____

 Encounter

Every encounter is a loving opportunity to
transform, even when the encounter is negative.
Negativity is a perception; positive is a perception.
Positive and negative are a pair; encountering both is a part of life.
Encountering both is a part of life.
They both can lead to opportunities of love.

Date:_____

 Needle

The only way to string a needle is through the eye.
Means some things are the way they are, like stringing a needle.
Accepting it as such sometimes is the best
way you can work with that thing.
Work with that thing as if stringing a needle.

Date:_____

To Know

Know that there is more to life than
can be seen with the regular perception.
This deeper inner knowing is the ancient magical mystery
of life and living. To know is to become.
Only in becoming, can one truly know.
Start the journey of learning knowing today.
Learning knowing today is to know.

Date:_____

_____

_____

_____

_____

_____

_____

_____

_____

_____

_____

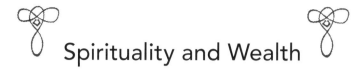

Spirituality and Wealth

Authentic wealth mirrors spirituality, and health.
Staying inside and outside one's self
consistently aligning with source, spirit, positive energy, love,
and joy is the key to manifesting wealth in positive affluence.
Spirit mirrors heaven, physical wealth mirrors earth, and body.
Be mindful of greed as you balancing heaven and earth.
Balancing heaven and earth through love, joy and light,
is every human's quest. Every human's quest is bringing
heaven's spirituality and wealth to earth as a positive resource
for spirit, wealth, and abundant health.

Date:_____

Cloud Creation

Clouds change from moment to moment.
Two soft clouds connecting strongly can create lightening.
Many soft clouds can create gentle showers or thunderstorms.
Rain falls down not up. Clouds rain down to shower and cleanse
everything. Bathing, and quenching the mother earth's thirst.
Mother earth is no longer thirsty. Feeding her, she then creates
everything for all living things to survive, grow, and move.
In recycling the rain, the mother earth with ease, willingly gives
back the water that she does not digest in her belly. This water
evaporates up again, which then creates more clouds,
and then rains again and again.

Again, and again the creative forces of nature is an ever wonderful
blooming, gifted creation. Creatively giving, and recycling with every
breath and movement. Even cloud is a wonderful blessing in the
dance of life and cloud creation.

Date:_____

 Stop The Ocean

How do you stop the ocean from moving?
This is a silly question. You cannot stop the ocean from moving
unless the earth, and the whole universe stop moving.
The ocean follows the rhythm and vibration of the earth's
universal movement. The Ocean's movements back and forth
are a universal unconditional commitment, bonded in sacred union.
Bonded in sacred union, you should not think of stopping the ocean
because nothing but the universal force of divine source can stop the ocean.

Date:_____

_____

_____

_____

_____

_____

_____

_____

_____

_____

_____

_____

_____

The Water Flows

The water flows without hesitation.
Without hesitation and with confidence, the water trusts its flow.
Trust its flow that whatever lies in its path will be ok.
The water flows around, over, and through. Around, over,
and through, the river flows downhill, with a lazy dance.
With a lazy dance the river trusts with diligent power, confidence,
and acceptance. You can practice mirroring the flow of the water;
follow the flow of diligent power, trust, confidence, and acceptance.
The river goes to find its friend the ocean; knowingly the water flows.

Date:_____

Rain Drops

Rain drops falling upon the blanket of the waves in the ocean.
Rain drops falling on the waves like water falling on moving glass.
Like water falling on moving glass, waves in ocean are solid and lucid.
Waves in ocean are solid, and lucid; flexibly, and penetratingly
absorbing the rain drops. Rain drops absorbing waves, waves
absorbing rain drops. Waves absorbing rain drops, and turtles.
Turtles swimming in ocean absorbing rain drops. Turtles, raindrops,
and ocean flowing interconnected, and effortlessly. Interconnected
and effortlessly the sun rises from behind the rainless
clouds to smile at rain drops in ocean, waves, and turtles.
Ocean, rain drops and turtle embraces the sun.
It is sunny; no more rain drops.

Date:_____

_____

_____

_____

_____

_____

_____

_____

_____

_____

_____

_____

 Judgment

When there is no judgment everything can become effortless.
Effortless like the hummingbird, taking the nectar out of
beautiful flowers. Arriving at golden opportunities
of life and living. Receiving golden opportunities for
living life in love, joy, nectar, and bliss.
You can choose to effortlessly take a break from judgment.

Date:_____

A Secret

There is a secret that lies in the emptiness of all things.
The secret is that everything lies in the emptiness of all things.
Emptiness has the full potential of form.
Form has full potential for emptiness, and everything.
Everything is waiting to be explored as a magical secret.
A magical secret of life is a secret.

Date:_____

Coming

To forget where you are coming from is to forget where you are. Forgetting where you are, and not being able to value the present. Valuing the present moment as you experience life helps you naturally to remember the past. The past is in the present, and the future is in the present. So there is less forgetting the past and the future if you can stay in the moment, and experience the coming.

Date:_____

No Noise

When the noise inside you quiets down;
then the noise outside you will quiet down as well.
As well, there will be silence in, and out, and no more noise.

A Bridge

There is no way to cross a bridge half way.
The cloudy sky can be as pleasant as the cloudless sky.
It depends on the person's perception as they cross a bridge.

Date:_____

_____

_____

_____

_____

_____

_____

_____

_____

_____

_____

_____

_____

Wheel of Life

To master the wheel of life is to
clear the ancient pathways within yourself of any toxic imprints;
giving the pathways up to renewed transformative light.
Renewed, and transformed you can jump more effortlessly
into the void of light, to serve as you wish. To serve as you wish,
assisting yourself, and others unconditionally to improve their pathways.
To become a master guide you must first know, live, experience,
and practice the pathways of light. In practicing the pathways of light,
part of the long-term practice is to cultivate humility to balance the
powers of light. The powers of light will assist the wheel of life
in turning, evolving, and transforming more effortlessly. One mirroring
the other, serving, and assisting the other. By assisting and serving
one another as humans, we assist and serve all living things,
the Universe, and Source. Infinitely we then
maintain ancient pathways within
ourselves, and in universal ways as well. As well continuously back
to the infinite void again, and again, the wheel of life continues to turn.
Continues to turn expanding, and expanding the infinite Source grows, and
evolves. Evolving and transforming, the endless journey continues
through the gateless gates of the wheel of life.

Date:_____

_____

_____

_____

_____

_____

_____

_____

_____

_____

_____

_____

_____

 Everything

Everything is everything, everything is within everything.
Everything is within you, you are within everything.
Everything's authentic nature is love, light, and emptiness.
Emptiness is everything like void within infinite space.
Infinite space and no time is everything.

Date:_____

_____

_____

_____

_____

_____

_____

_____

_____

_____

_____

_____

_____

_____

Energy Equals

Energy equals Creator-God-Universal Source, and
Hu-Wo-Man as a mirror. Everything is energy, and a reflection
of the energy created within. Every action creates an energy imprint,
and a reaction that is mirrored back to everything.
Everything equals energy. Energy equals everything.

Date:_____

_____

_____

_____

_____

_____

_____

_____

_____

_____

_____

_____

_____

Void

The original nature of everything is void: empty. There is no up or down.
There is no front or back. There is no right side or left side. What I am trying
to say is that names, and conditions of awareness,
are rational, human-created
processes through the alphabet, scientific
rational intellect, and human-created
mathematics. These created processes are
labels of human's attempt to control,
manipulate, identify, file, calculate, separate,
multiply, divide, add, simplify,
interconnect and organize what they can
perceive. These perceptions are only
a limited view of what infinitely exists, and that which continuously changes
within every second. These created human processes limit all things, and our
experiences of what authentically exist.
What exists is pure limitless infinite empty
space of unlimited potential. Authentic unlimited intelligent wisdom
created consistently by the Source.

Are you listening? Everything is a big zero,
null, empty. Empty and waiting to be
discovered and used with love, and light, like
a beautiful treasure. Like a beautiful
treasure life begins and never ends. Everything
is energy and cannot be destroyed,

but can be transformed. Our constant busyness
to make it otherwise keeps us
occupied from our infinite authentic potential
and responsibility. Try to make the
busyness less, and create some stillness time
to figure out what is your personal
responsibility to improve yourself, and then
to share, if you can, with others.
Love and light can be found and created within the emptiness of **Void.**

Date:_____

_____

_____

_____

_____

_____

_____

_____

_____

_____

_____

_____

_____

Equality

If you genuinely improve the quality of life for
anyone, or anything, your life will receive the same in return.
Remember life (and living) is a mirror, a mirror of
limitless equality of time and space, and no time and no space.
The mirror of life mirrors equality.

Date:_____

Unity of Heaven and Earth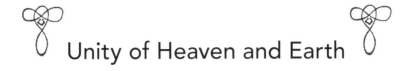

Unity of heaven and earth, masculine and feminine,
light and dark, can create divine unity. This divine unity
can maximize human's potential for evolution and growth.
Evolution and growth can improve, and unite heaven and earth.

Date:_____

Essential Inner Qualities

There are many essential qualities to inner peace,
spiritual growth, and personal development.
Some of these inner qualities that can be cultivated within are:
unconditional love, peace, silence, wisdom, joy, honor, dedication,
humility, patience, discipline, integrity, passion, kindness,
gratitude, compassion, giving, receiving, trust, and confidence.
Yes, when negative attitudes and lifestyles are transformed, you
can cultivate or create from within these essential inner qualities.

Date:_____

_____

_____

_____

_____

_____

_____

_____

_____

_____

_____

_____

_____

Basic Nature

Part of the perceived basic nature of human potential are love, light, darkness, and fear. Darkness and fear are mirrors of the absence of love and light. The more love and light are cultivated the less darkness and fear can become. It is your choice and responsibility to create what you feel or think is right for you. Enjoy whatever you choose to create. Creating and balancing love and light, and darkness and fear, are part of your basic nature.

Date:_____

_____

_____

_____

_____

_____

_____

_____

_____

_____

_____

_____

An Artist

Being an artist allows what shows up to just be.
Being creatively beautiful just being an artist
without judgment as you create will in its
own way show up to be an artist.

Smile

Smile! the sun is shining, the moon is glowing,
and the stars are out. Also, maybe when it is cloudy,
and raining, you can smile.

Date:_____

Compassion

The greatest compassion one can have is the compassion
and unconditional love someone gives to an enemy
or someone they do not like. Compassion, forgiveness,
and unconditional love are of the cultivated art of positively
improving spiritually, mentally, emotionally, and physically.
These compassionate practices can assist in purifying, and healing.
Healing compassionately is to gracefully understand.
Gracefully understand and practice the path of love and compassion.

Date:_____

Walking Along The Beach

Walking along the beach, the sun was shining sparkling overhead. My body and mind had spent the last three days peeling away the layers of tiredness. In meditation I discovered a part of myself that was always there. This forgotten part of myself arrived from within me and it said, "Hi there, I have not seen you in a while." The lightest, deepest part of my spirit, and my spirit's mind. A part I had not seen, or experienced consistently since a young child from birth to seven years old. My first seven years of lightness, and beauty. Lightness and beauty an essence of innocent connection to my spirit's mind, and body. I felt at peace and totally connected. Feeling this presence of myself, I decided to sit in silence. In silence I became very aware of the presence of Source energy within me. Source energy within me, in me bonded before birth, bonded at birth, bonded after birth, bonded as I experience life, and living, bonding at death and after death. I come to realize that this part of me can never be lost, just sometimes consciously forgotten. This inner energy Source part of me said again, "Hi, welcome home, welcome home to your beautiful essence of spirit, woman, human, and creator." Tears of joy ran down my cheeks; the inner child was acknowledged and at peace. At peace and with equanimity I said, " Welcome." I got up and walked along the beach.

Date:_____

 The Waves

Moving, moving, moving, Splash!
Waves expressing colors of green, light blue and deep blue.
The waves moving up, back, forward, down, and side to side.
Making sounds of splash, shissh, chee, slurp.
The waves tireless moving small, big, bigger
Making sounds of Splash, chee, plop, shee, and rolling.
Everyone different, they foam, they roll, they push, they pull.
Riding over one another they dance together, and separate.
Rippling, and bouncing smaller waves, big waves. But are
they small or big; or, are they just waves. Waves
working together as a whole to keep the momentum.
Keeping the momentum of ebb and flow of the planet, creating
balance, and alignment. In balance and alignment every wave's
movement reflects unconditionally dedicated love. Love that is
not separate, no better, no different, all interconnected are the waves.

Date:_____

_____

_____

_____

_____

_____

_____

_____

_____

_____

_____

_____

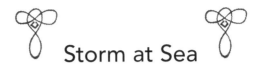 Storm at Sea

Sea creatures huddle together darkness spilled over the violent waves.
The waves hurry to spit out different sizes of tree limbs, coconut,
cord, coral, plastic and sand. Emptying wave
by wave, the waste collected from
the violent storm spills forth, in, and around
the sea, and on the sandy shore.
No moon, no stars in the sky, only darkness, wind, water, and
the crashing sounds of the debris and waves.
The waves carried more and more
to shore sea creatures, and much giant debris. Sea creatures and debris
landing on shore more and more, resting, tired from the storm at sea.

Date:_____

_____

_____

_____

_____

_____

_____

_____

_____

_____

_____

_____

_____

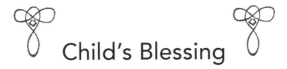 Child's Blessing

You have come to light your parents' way like a star in the sky,
and a full moon on a pleasant night. May your journey in your
mother's womb be filled with pleasant experiences, yummy food,
restful days and heartfelt pleasantries. May your journey as you enter
this planet be effortless, clear, and interesting. Please take time on the
path of your birth to stop and smell the roses. May your journey onward
after you have entered the planet, be one of health, wisdom, creativity,
joy, peace, harmony, loyalty, honesty, respect, and prosperity.
Within you and outside you, may love, light, and many blessings
be effortlessly your choice. May three Swans be your foundation
as you journey through your life, and beyond.

Date:_____

Tea

See the Tea. See what it looks like to you.
Hear; listen to the stories of its journey as
your luscious lips embrace the cup.
Smell its cranberry, apple favors; woven together with the generous
interweaving of the water. Let the smell fill your
body and soul from head to toes.
Taste its favors from the earths' warm, succulent womb of creation.
Feel! Feel the tea's warm embrace as it flows
into your mouth, rolls down your
throat, caressing its inner walls. Passing through to your heart, your
bosom of love's embrace. Your stomach
awakens, embracing as the tea gently
arrives into the bottom of your stomach. Your
stomach peacefully embracing
the tea with love and delight. With love and delight let your
whole body smile with warm shivers of delightful tea.

Date:_____

_____

_____

_____

_____

_____

_____

_____

_____

_____

_____

_____

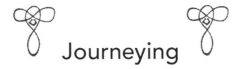 Journeying

Once we are born we must die. Everything dies.
Live in every moment as if it were the last moment.
Honor and cherish respectfully your journey with
humility and mindfulness. With humility, mindfulness, and
respect, enjoy each experience and step along the path as you
journey. As you journey, leave no unfinished step.
Mindfully completing each step, taking nothing for granted, the
endless, gateless path continues. The endless, gateless path continues
until the footsteps become invisible. With trust, the invisible path
can create more love, light, and joy. With love, light, and joy, the
path becomes much clearer and filled with integrity.
Once we are born we must journey.
Once we die we must journey.
How I choose, I will journey.

Date:_____

Rambling Awareness

The kind of courage it takes to heal is the courage that transcends fear. Truth is telling it as it is. Not turning the "is" into what you would like "is" to become. The Source dwells within you as You. So choose to create consciously and mindfully. Originally you are a sacred space of light; try to empty fear and recreate light, giving rebirth to your original divine self. The brain is like two sets of lovers embracing at the top of infinity within no space, and no time. My body gives my spirit a platform to express itself. Pure darkness without fear is like night. Like night it supports and holds unconditionally the emptiness of light, as night in the moment. The root of your being is invisible and is connected to the Source like a drop of water and a grain of sand returning to the ocean.

The spirit and the physical essence of the herbs in the vase caressed my eyesight with exuberant passion. Awakened and alive the herbs shimmer, as if slightly trembling to my presence. I continue to embrace the herbs in the vase with my eyes; I wonder am I seeing this or is it only my perception through my eyes. "What does it matter?" I think, "It just is."

When someone receives healing treatment to transform symptoms of imbalances or negative situations, they must also take responsibility to make decisions to transform old maps of negative personal attitudes, imprints of trauma or perceived suffering, habits of being a part of career or personal stressful situations, and lifestyle environmental stressors that supported and assisted in creating the negative imbalances.

Healing treatments are tools. Healing treatments do not magically erase all the problems and symptoms of imbalances. The treatments can assist in improving the situation. Improving the imbalance long-term depends on the person's transformational choices. Sometimes it can take a combination of many healing tools to long-term improve the imbalance. From my professional and personal experiences, all healing tools can be useful if the person takes the time and responsibility to create the change and transformation to the new map they seek.

When humans stress their positive light and life force, energy becomes depleted or decreases. This decrease of light and life force energy can continue based on the level of stress, how long the situation continues, and if the person is doing something to improve the quality of their light and life force energy. The longer the person keeps the stressors and negative imprints within their energy system, mind, emotion, and physical body, the more the stressors take root and get stronger. After some time, these stressors and imprints create disharmony and imbalances that can express themselves in many different ways.

All healing and transformation can only holistically and successfully happen from within you. Energy healing treatments of any kind, teachers, guides, shamans, healers, anyone or anything outside of the person, can only help or assist. They cannot completely do the healing for the person. The person must take responsibility to choose and work on what they would like to transform for complete or long-term balance to occur. Seeking help or assistance when necessary, and exploring all avenues for healing and transforming the situation is recommended. What is hidden in the dark must come to the light for improved healing and transformation to occur. You must live the change you see in order to have the vibration of your chosen transformed desires.

Someone assisting others professionally or personally in transforming negative stressors, patterns, trauma, attitudes, or imbalances must work on themselves first before assisting others. If this is not done, the facilitator assisting can create more imbalances to the client, and to himself as well. The practitioner or facilitator is the channel for the process, and the quality of the assistance to the client can be affected by the practitioner's or facilitator's personal transformation, experience, and wisdom of the skills he is using as a tool. Someone cannot give what he does not have. Everything is your choice. Choices give options. Options can create peace, improvements, well-being, balance, and harmony.

When someone becomes fearless of fear and darkness, fear and darkness can become empty of negative frequencies. The person is then free by choice to embrace love and light. This journey on a sacred path of love and light takes patience, commitment, courage, responsibility, diligence, and self-love. This is a journey and process within to discover the realms of possibilities. The further in the person goes to transform negative vibrations the person becomes more and more unmasked. The peeling away of many layers of what is chosen to transform can create a natural nervousness and a sense of being scared. This natural nervousness and sense of being scared is normal because the person becomes more conscious of arriving into unfamiliar places of more grace, love and more light. Now the person has to get used to this unfamiliar situation and then create new comfort levels of embracing where they are, and possibly where they are going.

These new pathways within can sometimes seem invisible, which can be perceived as unknown, very silent, lonely, and a strange feeling of sadness that is also experienced as joyous. After some time, contentment, trust, faith, joy, grace, love and light evolve into a welcoming habit. Connected and content, using genuine faith and trust, the sacred path that leads to more emptiness, positive growth, and awakening, reveals itself and becomes more and more accepted. Soon you can feel yourself riding the positive energies of love and light like a horse and rider. The transformation continues as the letting go of the past negativity continues, arriving at a more and more silent journey of focus, contentment, concentration, peace, and meditation. The person can choose to continue as they wish. As they wish, the infinite journey within continues to unfold like a flower.

Humans have the potential to open and evolve like a flower, transforming into cultivating a magical garden of more love and light. You are the gardener of your garden, so you can choose wisely to dream and create consciously the seeds that you would like to plant and enjoy in your garden of life.

Remember from within you, all humans have infinite potential, and humans have a natural tendency to want to be a part of love and light.

See you again!

I wish you all the best with everything on your Sacred Journey of Spirit.

Biography

Dorothea Orleen Grant was born in Montego Bay, Jamaica, West Indies. She has two children Renea, and Pia; and a granddaughter Ayanna. Dorothea's professional career training and degrees are; Business Management from Duff's Business College in Jamaica, three General Manager Certifications in different restaurant operations USA, Metaphysics from the American Institute of Holistic Theology USA, Meditation from Zen Master Thich Nhat Hanh and the Monks and Nuns of Plum Village, and professional training in the ancient energy healing arts of the Incas Shaman, Healer, Sage, from the Four Winds Society, and the Inca shamans of the Sacred Valley, and Amazon in Peru. Dorothea is also a certified traditional Reiki Grand Master Teacher. Currently Dorothea uses her authentic talents and professional training in the holistic energy healing arts at Dogca Universal Wellness, a center she created in 2000. This healing arts center is located in Midland Park, New Jersey.

Throughout Dorothea's life, the art of storytelling and writing is also a natural talent, and passion. She enjoys the magic of dreaming, and weaving vibrations with her writing skills from the non-physical to the physical, with the intention of taking people to places they might not be able to go in their normal human perception. Dorothea is the author of "Chakras" Introduction To The Seven Major Energy Centers, and two guided meditation CDs "Sacred Activation" and "Deep Relaxation."

Notes

Notes

Notes